Goldilocks and the Three Bears

Goldlöckchen und die drei Bären

First published 2024 by Mooliprint

© 2024 Mooliprint

ISBN 978-1-915963-20-8

All rights reserved.

Without limiting the rights under copyright reserved above, no part of this publication may be reproduced, stored in a retrieval system, or transmitted in any form or by any means, electronic, mechanical, photocopying, recording or otherwise, without the prior permission of the publisher.

Once upon a time, there were three bears. A Papa Bear, a Mama Bear and a Baby Bear.

Es waren einmal drei Bären. Papa Bär, Mama Bär und Baby Bär.

One day, Papa Bear made some delicious porridge but it was too hot so they went out for a long walk to let the porridge cool.

Eines Tages kochte Papa Bär einen leckeren Brei, aber er war zu heiß, also machten sie einen langen Spaziergang, um den Brei abkühlen zu lassen.

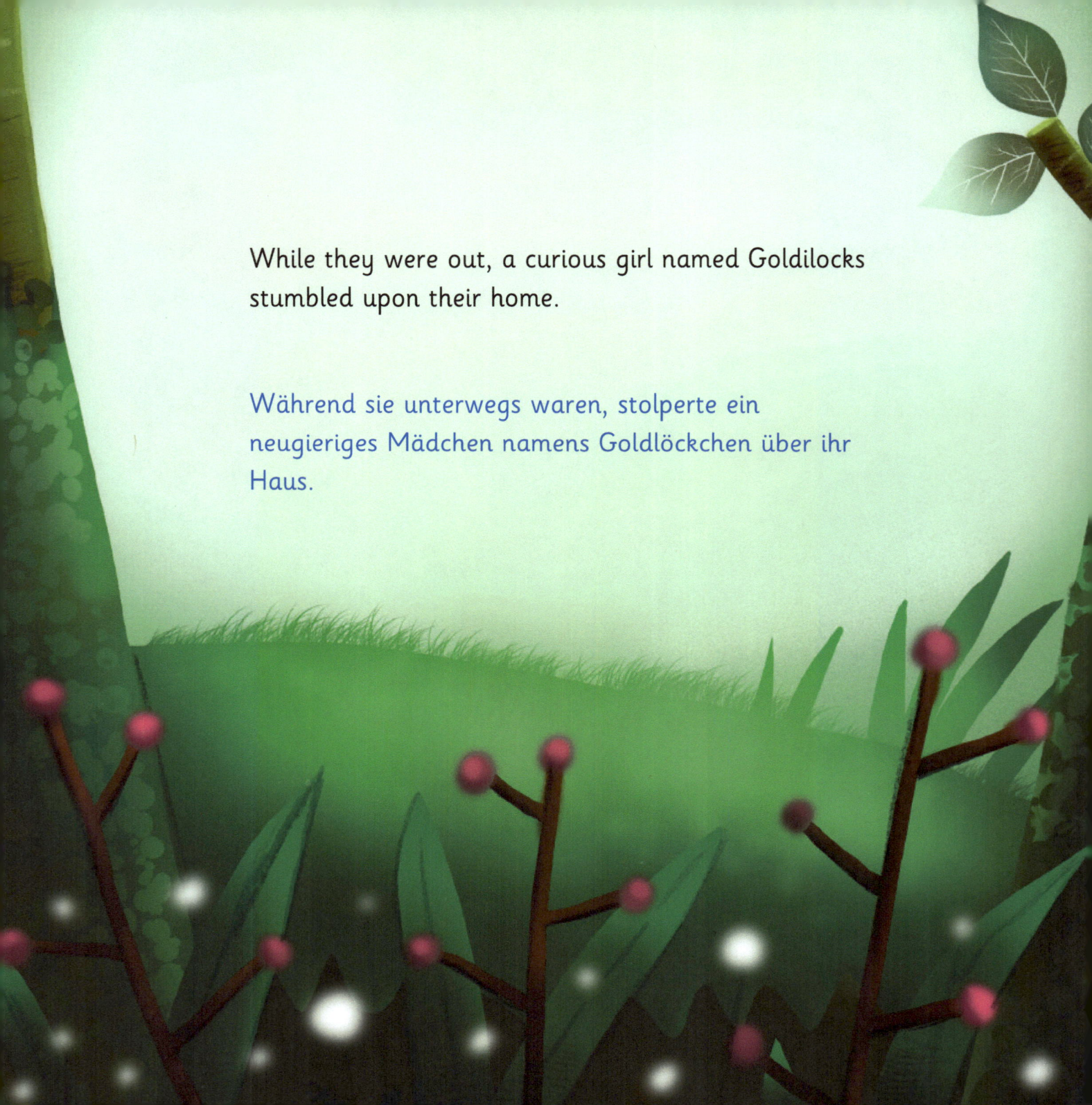

While they were out, a curious girl named Goldilocks stumbled upon their home.

Während sie unterwegs waren, stolperte ein neugieriges Mädchen namens Goldlöckchen über ihr Haus.

Finding the door unlocked, she entered, drawn by the smell of porridge.

Als sie die Tür unverschlossen vorfand, trat sie ein, angezogen vom Geruch des Breis.

She tasted the porridge from the three bowls on the table.
Papa Bear's porridge was too hot.

Sie probierte den Brei aus den drei Schüsseln auf dem Tisch.
Papa Bärs Brei war zu heiß.

Mama Bear's too cold, but Baby Bear's was just right, so she ate it all up!

Der von Mama Bär war zu kalt, aber der von Baby Bär war genau richtig, also aß sie alles auf!

After eating, Goldilocks felt tired and explored the house further, finding three chairs in the living room. She tried sitting in all of them.

Nach dem Essen fühlte sich Goldlöckchen müde, erkundete das Haus weiter und fand drei Stühle im Wohnzimmer. Sie versuchte, sich auf alle zu setzen.

Papa Bear's chair was too hard, Mama Bear's chair was too soft, but Baby Bear's chair was just right. Unfortunately, when she sat on it, the chair broke into pieces!

Der Stuhl von Papa Bär war zu hart, der von Mama Bär zu weich, aber der Stuhl von Baby Bär war genau richtig. Leider brach der Stuhl in Stücke, als sie sich darauf setzte!

Feeling even more tired, Goldilocks went upstairs to the bedroom, where she found three beds. She lay down in Papa Bear's bed, but it was too hard. Then she tried Mama Bear's bed, but it was too soft. Finally, she tried Baby Bear's bed, and it was just right. Goldilocks fell fast asleep.

Weil Goldlöckchen sich noch müder fühlte, ging sie nach oben ins Schlafzimmer, wo sie drei Betten fand. Sie legte sich in Papa Bärs Bett, aber es war zu hart. Dann probierte sie das Bett von Mama Bär, aber es war zu weich. Schließlich probierte sie das Bett von Baby Bär, und es war genau richtig. Goldlöckchen schlief schnell ein.

Meanwhile, the three bears returned home to find that someone had been eating their porridge. Papa Bear noticed his spoon had moved.

In der Zwischenzeit kamen die drei Bären nach Hause und mussten feststellen, dass jemand ihren Brei gegessen hatte. Papa Bär bemerkte, dass sein Löffel bewegt worden war.

Mama Bear saw her porridge had been tasted, and Baby Bear cried, "Someone ate all my porridge!"

Mama Bär sah, dass ihr Brei gekostet worden war, und Baby Bär weinte: „Jemand hat meinen ganzen Brei gegessen!"

Then, they saw that someone had been sitting in their chairs.
Papa Bear saw his chair was disturbed.

Dann sahen sie, dass jemand auf ihren Stühlen gesessen hatte.
Papa Bär sah, dass sein Stuhl verrückt worden war.

Mama Bear noticed the cushion on her chair had moved, and Baby Bear found his chair was completely broken!

Mama Bär bemerkte, dass das Kissen auf ihrem Stuhl verrutscht war, und Baby Bär stellte fest, dass sein Stuhl ganz kaputt war!

They moved quietly upstairs where they discovered Papa Bear's blanket had been moved.

Sie gingen leise nach oben, wo sie entdeckten, dass Papa Bärs Decke verrutscht war.

Mama Bear's pillow was squashed, but to their surprise they found Goldilocks sleeping in Baby Bear's bed. At the sound of their voices, she woke up!

Mama Bärs Kissen war zerdrückt, aber zu ihrer Überraschung fanden sie Goldlöckchen schlafend in Baby Bärs Bett. Als sie ihre Stimmen hörten, wachte sie auf!

She jumped out of bed and ran all the way home.

The three bears lived happily ever after in their little house in the forest, always remembering to lock their door when they went out.

Sie sprang aus dem Bett und rannte den ganzen Weg nach Hause.

Die drei Bären lebten glücklich und zufrieden in ihrem kleinen Haus im Wald und vergaßen nicht, die Tür abzuschließen, wenn sie hinausgingen.

As for Goldilocks, she learned to never enter someone's house without permission.

Und Goldlöckchen lernte, dass man niemals ohne Erlaubnis das Haus eines anderen betreten sollte.

Find the name of the bears
Finde den Namen der Bären

Mama Bear / Bär

Baby Bear / Bär

Papa Bear / Bär

Help Goldilocks get home!

Hilf Goldlöckchen, nach Hause zu kommen!

Spot the difference

Finde den Unterschied

There are 6 to find

Es gibt 6 zu finden

Answers

Antworten

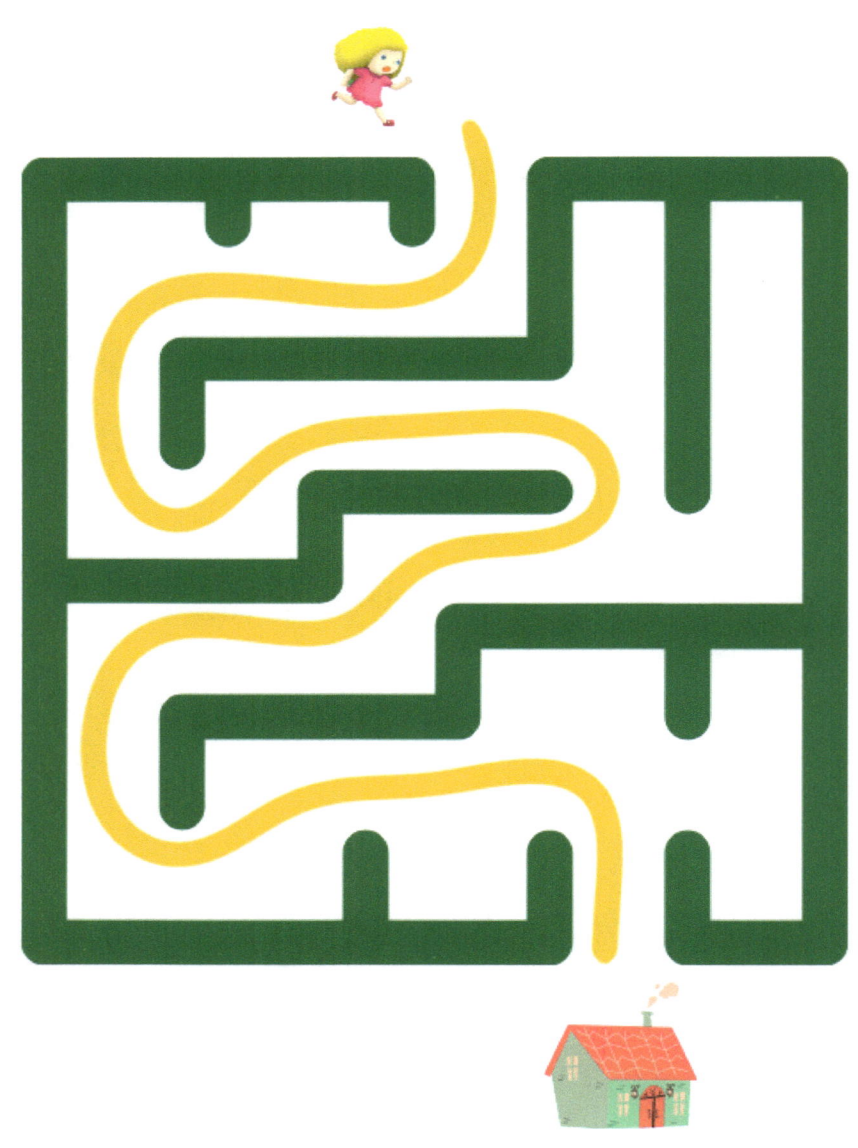

FREE GERMAN AUDIO BOOK!

Unlock the captivating audio version of Goldlöckchen und die drei Bären by signing up for my newsletter. Be the first to hear about new releases and enjoy exclusive discounts!

visit https://dl.bookfunnel.com/b104wa5h9m or scan the QR code

to find more bilingual books visit

BILINGUAL BOOKS

www.mooliprint.com

www.ingramcontent.com/pod-product-compliance
Lightning Source LLC
Chambersburg PA
CBHW041126130526
44590CB00054B/56